THE
Justin
Wilson

COOKBOOK

PELICAN PUBLISHING COMPANY
GRETNA 2013

DEDICATION

To my wife, Sara, whom I call Mama. An' she's a dam' good cook, also, too, I garontee!

First printing, 1965
Reprinted three times
First Pelican edition, October 1975
Second printing, November 1979
Third printing, March 1982
Fourth printing, August 1983
Fifth printing, May 1984
Sixth printing, May 1985
Seventh printing, January 1986
Eighth printing, December 1986
Ninth printing, November 1988
Tenth printing, May 1990
Eleventh printing, March 1992
Twelfth printing, March 2002
Thirteenth printing, September 2003
Fourteenth printing, July 2007
Fifteenth printing, February 2010
Sixteenth printing, January 2013

Library of Congress Cataloging in Publication Data

Wilson, Justin
    The Justin Wilson cookbook.

    1. Cookery, American — Louisiana. 2. Cookery,
Creole. I. Title.
TX715.W7492 1979   641.5'9763   79-20070
ISBN-13: 978-0-88289-019-7

Printed in the United States of America

Published by Pelican Publishing Company, Inc.
1000 Burmaster Street, Gretna, Louisiana 70053

CONTENTS

FOREWORD

Me, I'm in love!

With cookin', that is, in case Sara is readin' this.

An' I done got me this love affair more years behind than I like to confess, although I an't nearly so ol' as some peoples think I is!

Mos' especially, I'm in love with cookin' Cajun-style, since I done brought myself up among these wondermous people, the Louisiana Cajuns.

What I love mos' about Cajun cookin' is the imagines what they done put into it.

You see, my frien', although some Cajuns is rich as thick cream, mos' of them ain't what you would call broke out with riches, I garontee. An' mos' of them Cajuns ain't got the money to buy them fancy cuts of meat and high price' vegetables. An' that's where the imagines comes in.

Down through the centuries, the Louisiana Cajun, like his French cousin, has learned to improvise, usin' the less expensive meats an' vegetables in they cookin'.

There is certain––how you call it––staples what the Cajun cooks with mos' ever' day of his life. Stuff like rice, corn meal, red beans, peas, okra, tomatoes an' eggplant.

Cajuns cook a lot of chicken, pork, cheap cuts of beef and lamb. An', bein' some of the most greates' hunters in the worl', they also eat lots of rabbit, squirrel, venison, 'coon an' mushrat.

But maybe the most bes' things the Cajun cooks is things like shrimp, catfish, crabs, oysters an' turtle, what he usually catch hisself.

Now, mos' anybody can cook a meal if they can read readin'. An' there is lots of good cook books what you can buy.

But this little cook book is somethin' different. It ain't exactly––how you call it––a ''beginners'' book. It ain't gonna tol' you how to boil a egg or cook a steak.

Howsomever, there ain't a recipe in this book that you can't cook––an' good, too, providin' you got the right attitude.

The right attitude is made up from two things: You' imagines and you' common ol' horse sense, of which the Cajun has hisself a barrel of. If you looks on cookin' as fun, which it sure can be, you got you'self a runnin' start on becomin' a Cajun cook.

Once you learn to make a fine roux, to boil rice, to make barbecue sauce from scratch an' to use the seasonin's you find in this book, then cookin' Cajun-style is gonna become fun, I garontee.

An' you gonna learn how to use wine in you' cookin'. A little sauterne, a little claret, sometime a little sherry can make a mos' ordinair' dish taste like somethin' cooked by angels.

If you got the prohibits about wine, don' you worry none. The alcohol done cook itse'f right out of that pot in jus' ten or nine seconds. An' all what you got lef' is that wondermous flavor.

But the real basic thing about Cajun cookin' is still imagines an' common sense, I garontee.

You' imagines eventually gonna tell you to add a little somethin' here, a little somethin' there, to these recipes. 'Sperimentin' gonna come easy pretty soon.

You' common sense gonna tell you what goes good with what, an' when, too. You gonna know you don't put you' sawmill gravy on them prunes.

So, one of these days, you gonna cast you' eye over somethin' you is cookin' an you gonna reallyize that you is a good Cajun cook. Maybe not so good like Uncle Justin, but good!

An' that day maybe ain't too far off when you gonna discover that you usin' all five of you' senses when you cook.

You' taste sense is the first big one. Then you' smell sense, he come on big. An' you eye sense come along pretty fas' too. Even you' feel sense gonna come in handy, time to time.

But one day or so, you gonna caught you'self listenin' to see if you' rice is finish cook or not.

That gonna be the day you gonna yell ''Hoo, boy, I finally is a Cajun cook, for sure!''

An' that the day I pray for you to get to. 'Cause that the day you' gonna start really gettin' you' enjoys from cookin'.

Me, I done eaten every dish in this little book maybe four or three hundred times. An' it make me sad for you because you been missin' so much all you' life.

So, here is you' own Justin Wilson Cook Book. Bon soir! Bon appetit! You' gonna have the time from you' life, I garontee!:

October 1, 1965   **JUSTIN WILSON,** Pete's Highway, Denham Springs, Louisiana

HOW TO MAKE A ROUX

The "roux" is the foundation of many, many Cajun dishes. You will find it referred to in a number of the recipes in this book.

The "roux" which follows is the one I have used for many years, with great success-- I garontee!

ROUX

1½ cups sifted flour   Olive oil

Cover bottom of heavy pot with olive oil. After the olive oil is well heated over a slow fire, add the flour. Cook the flour very slowly, stirring almost constantly. The flour must be browned to a very dark brown, nearly black, but not actually burned.

This takes more time than you might think is necessary but a good "roux" must be cooked slowly to get all floury taste out of it and to insure uniformity of color. This is the basic "roux."

Although all "roux" are pretty much the same in Cajun kitchens, there are variations practiced by some stubborn ol' cooks which I won't attempt to go into here.

However, as you read this book, you'll see where several recipes call for a couple of additional ingredients.

For instance, after you have made the basic "roux" you can add a small can of tomato paste, stirring this all the time until the "roux" has reached the color of the flour before the paste was added. Then add a small can of tomato sauce, stirring this into the mixture until it all turns dark brown again.

My papa, the late Harry D. Wilson, he done said one time he jus' as soon eat a pine burr as a artichoke. So nex' time I fix this recipe, he got himse'f a pine burr on his plate.

An' I ain' gonna tell you what he said 'bout that, 'cause this book paper done burn right up if I do.

But when he try this recipe, he change his mind and from then on he fightin' for his burr artichoke, jus' like the rest of us.

APPETIZERS AND DIPS

BOILED BURR ARTICHOKES

2 to 4 fresh young burr artichokes
¾ cup olive oil
1 large onion, quartered
2 large cloves garlic
3 to 4 cups claret or sauterne
    wine

Louisiana Red Hot Sauce
1 tablespoon Lea & Perrins
    Worcestershire
Salt
Water
¼ cup lemon juice

Wash artichokes well and let them drain. Put in pot large enough for liquids to cover them, or nearly so. Pour olive oil over them and put onions, lemon juice and garlic in pot. Pour wine over artichokes and add Louisiana Hot Sauce and Worcestershire. Add enough water to get desired amount of liquid. Salt to taste. Cook covered over medium flame, adding additional water as needed. It is not necessary, however, to keep the artichokes covered with liquid when they near completion of cooking. Cook until outside leaves are very tender. After artichokes are done, keep them covered so they will steam for about thirty minutes. Cool or chill and serve.

Serves 4 to 8, depending on how artichoke hungry you are. Hell, I can eat all that myself, when I'm artichoke hungry!

Now some folks say it bad manners to dunk you' garlic bread in you' wine. An' I mus' admit this is good, even if you bite a big chunk of this bread and chase it with a little wine.

But me, I like to dunk an' I don' think dunkin' is bad, neither. An' it taste so good with you' meal, too.

So don't forgot, it ain't no sin to dunk. An' if it is, who give a dam' anyway?

GARLIC BREAD AU BEAUJOLAIS

2 Sticks butter
Pressed garlic or garlic puree
Romano or Parmesan cheese

Black ground pepper
Loaf of French bread
Beaujolais wine

Mix two sticks butter with either pressed garlic or garlic puree to taste. Add Romano or Parmesan cheese to the amount that it will still spread easily. Sprinkle with black ground pepper. Slice French bread into slices lengthwise. Spread garlic butter on generously. Toast in oven.

Dip garlic bread in Beaujolais wine when eating it. This is known as dunking and you will find that it is delicious. Don't mind the crumbs in your wine - you'll eat those too. Dunking should be done while eating your meal.

SMOKED SAUSAGE AND OYSTERS A LA JUSTIN

2 pounds country smoked
    sausage
1 quart medium sized fresh
    oysters
2 cups sauterne wine

1 teaspoon Louisiana Hot Sauce
½ teaspoon garlic salt
½ teaspoon salt
Juice from ½ lemon

Cut sausage in one inch pieces and place in large frying pan, preferably an iron one. Add oysters, wine, hot sauce, garlic salt, salt and lemon juice. Bring to a good boil. Then turn fire down so that it will cook slowly. Cook until most of the juice is gone, leaving just enough to serve as gravy if you wish. Be sure that sausage is well cooked and tender. Serves 6 to 8 either as an appetizer or as a dish for the meal.

"Mos' everyone gonna agree: They is shrimp, an' they is shrimp, an' they is shrimp. An' then they is Gulf Shrimp!"

SHRIMP DIP

2 pounds boiled shrimp
 coarsely ground
1 8 oz. package soft cream
 cheese
Juice of 1 lemon

10 green onions, minced
Mayonnaise
Hot sauce, Worcestershire
 sauce
Salt, pepper to taste

Soften cream cheese with lemon juice. Add shrimp and green onions to cream cheese mixture. Add enough mayonnaise to give a consistency for dipping potato chips or crackers. Season with hot sauce, Worcestershire sauce, salt and pepper. Much better if made eight hours prior to serving time. Add more seasoning if desired. About 15.

HOT SWISS 'N CIDER DIP

½ pound Swiss Processed
 Cheese, diced
1½ teaspoons of flour
1½ cups sweet apple cider or
 apple juice

½ teaspoon salt
⅛ teaspoon pepper
¼ teaspoon parsley or chives,
 finely chopped
Dash of garlic salt

Sprinkle diced cheese with flour. Heat cider to boiling point, then reduce heat to simmer. Add floured cheese, gradually stirring until all cheese is melted. Add seasoning. A good zippy dip used with toasted French bread wedges or potato chips. Serves about 15.

I want to tol' you something: If you don' look out, you gonna make this you' entree, because it is so good.

Don' you forgot to marinate them eggplant slices in salt water for a couple hours. If you don' did this, them eggplant might could be bitter. Sometime even the young ones is bitter if you don' did this.

EGGPLANT APPETIZER A LA JUSTIN

3 small eggplants
3 tablespoons olive oil
3 tablespoons sifted flour
1 small can tomato sauce
1 leaf celery, chopped fine
Small amount of chopped parsley
1 cup finely chopped onions
1 small, finely chopped bell pepper

1 clove finely chopped garlic
1 tablespoon Lea & Perrins
1 teaspoon Louisiana Hot Sauce
1¼ teaspoon salt
1½ cups claret wine
1 cup water (if needed)
Additional olive oil
2 cups grated Romano cheese

Peel eggplants and slice lengthwise in slices from ⅛ to ¼ inch thick. Place slices in salt water and let them marinate for about 2 hours. Rinse and place in colander to drain before starting next step. (While the eggplant is marinating, the rest of the recipe can be prepared.)

Make a roux with tomato sauce, (See Page 1). Next, add all the chopped seasoning celery, parsley, onions, bell pepper and garlic to roux, and cook over very low flame for about 20 - 30 minutes, stirring constantly. Add wine, Lea & Perrins and Louisiana Hot Sauce. Salt to taste, approximately 1¼ teaspoons. Add water if sauce is too thick. Cook on a slow fire for about one hour. When sauce is nearly done, put some olive oil in a frying pan and fry the drained eggplant slices to a deep brown. Place these slices on a platter and sprinkle Romano cheese freely. Then spread sauce freely over the slices. Do this to each layer of eggplant slices. Can be served hot or you may chill it in refrigerator, then slice like fudge and serve cold. Many prefer this way of serving. This recipe serves about eight persons as an appetizer.

When Sara an' me, we go to New Orleans sometime to hear Pete Fountain or maybe Al Hirt, we mos' usual stay at the Hotel Monteleone.

Sara an' me, we love that place! I mus' confess that the Monteleone merry-go-roun' bar done make me a little dizzy sometime, but it wort' it, I garontee!

But maybe what we love mos' at the Monteleone is they wondermous turtle soup.

After many years, me an' they chef got ourself acquaint' enough so he tell me how he make this turtle soup.

An' this recipe is it, only I done add jus' a little something here an' there, which I think even make it better. See if you don' agree with me, huh?

SOUPS AND SALADS

TURTLE SOUP A LA MONTELEONE

¾ gallon chicken stock
1 cup green onions, chopped fine
⅓ cup celery, chopped fine
   (do not use the leaves)
1 cup flour
1 cup tomato sauce

4 hard boiled eggs, chopped fine
¼ cup lemon, chopped fine
1 lb. turtle meat, all meat, no
   bones, cut in 1 inch cubes
Sherry wine

Prepare stock, saute onions and celery. Brown the flour, add flour to onions and celery. Mix into stock. Add tomato sauce, hard boiled eggs and lemon. Salt and pepper to taste.

Brown turtle meat, add to stock and cook over low flame for 2 hours, covered.

As you serve, add sherry wine to individual taste, not more than 1 tablespoon per bowl. Serves 12.

SALAD A LA WILSON

2 avocados
2 heaping tablespoons salad
   dressing
4 tablespoons olive oil

3 tablespoons wine vinegar
2 teaspoons Lea & Perrins
1 teaspoon Louisiana Hot Sauce
1 teaspoon salt

Peel and cut avocados in half. Mix well the other ingredients and pour over avocados.

"Who that say I don' got me a pot to cook in?--An' me, I got the window, too!"

RED BEAN SALAD

2 No. 3 cans beans
1 medium onion
1 cup celery
½ cup pickles, dill

2 hard boiled eggs
2 heaping tablespoons
   mayonnaise

Cook red beans or use canned ones—I prefer canned ones for this as they stay whole better. Drain well. Add chopped onions, celery, pickle, finely chopped eggs. Toss with mayonnaise. Salt and pepper to taste. I like a little Lea & Perrins and Louisiana Hot Sauce in this. Great with barbecue of any kind.

RED BEAN SOUP

See recipe for dry red beans or use any that are left over. After beans are cooked, mash well or put through a colander. Add water to consistency of thick soup. Serve with croutons.

FRENCH SALAD DRESSING A LA JUSTIN

1 medium clove of garlic
Salt
½ cup olive oil
½ lemon

¼ cup wine vinegar
2 teaspoons Lea & Perrins
½ teaspoon Louisiana Hot
   Sauce

Cover garlic amply with salt, mash with fork to fine pulp, taking up all of salt. Add olive oil, stir well. Add Lea & Perrins and hot sauce, stir well. Squeeze ½ lemon around sides so that it runs down into sauce. Stir well. Add wine vinegar, stir briskly.

Use on any green salad or tomato and lettuce. Serves 6.

"This li'l booney-cat Cajun already can count hisself up to 10 in French!"

COLD SLAW

1 large hard head of cabbage,
   shredded
2 medium onions, shredded into
   thin onion rings
5 heaping tablespoons mayonnaise
2 heaping tablespoons Durkees dressing

2 tablespoons olive oil
1 tablespoon wine vinegar
1 teaspoon Louisiana Hot Sauce
2 tablespoons catsup
½ to 1 teaspoon garlic salt
Juice of 1 lemon

Put mayonnaise and Durkees in a bowl large enough to hold complete mixture, but shaped so that it can be beaten with a fork. Beat mayonnaise and Durkees until combined, add olive oil slowly, beating all the while after adding olive oil. Beat until mixture has returned to thickness of original mayonnaise. Add Louisiana Hot Sauce, continuing to beat. Add catsup, keep beating. Add salt and garlic salt, beating all the time. Add wine vinegar; this will thin the sauce down. Beat this thoroughly, adding the lemon juice as you do so. Taste for salt and pepper, keeping in mind that you have to salt and pepper the slaw with this mixture. Therefore, it can be a little saltier than if you were just doing the sauce alone. Place shredded cabbage and onion rings in large salad bowl. Pour sauce over and toss well. This should be done about an hour before serving.

HOT SLAW

1 small cabbage (shredded)
1 large onion, chopped
1 bell pepper, chopped
2 cans whole tomatoes

2 strips bacon cut in small
   pieces
Red pepper
Salt and black pepper

Fry bacon until crisp—Saute onions and bell pepper until clear—Add cabbage and mix well. Add tomatoes, salt, red and black pepper to taste. Let simmer 45 minutes. (Some like to add 1 tablespoon vinegar for tartness.)

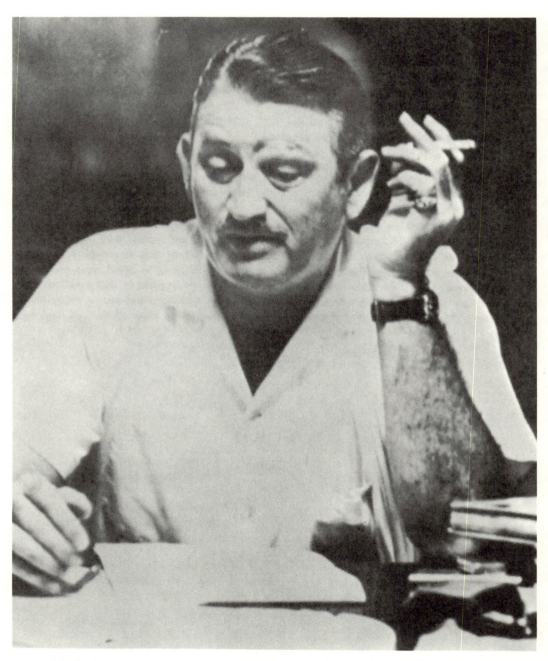

"Le's see now, was that one cup sauterne an' four clove garlic, or was that four cup sauterne an' one clove garlic?"

MARINATED GREEN BEANS

2 cans vertical packed green
  beans
2 medium onions (sliced)
French dressing

1 small wedge of blue cheese
1 small can pimento (cut in
  strips)

Make French Dressing, found on Page 13. Add the blue cheese that has been mashed and mix well. Put green beans, pimento and onions in a bowl and toss with this dressing. Cover and place in refrigerator overnight. Some people may not care for blue cheese and this can be eliminated. If any are left over, these can be added to a tossed green salad and are very good.

'Way back in the days befo' I made marriage wit' Sara, me an' my frien' Pierre Castille had us a big ol' house in Baton Rouge. An' us bachelors, we both like to cook some, I garontee! This recipe for baked cubed steak is one Pierre do from time to time. An' I want to tol' you that when he fix this, our friends——mostly the ladies——done stood in line, jus' waitin' to eat this dish. Now, you don' have to stood in line some at all! Jus' start cookin', raht now!

MEATS

BAKED CUBED STEAK

4 or 5 lbs. heavy beef steak,
   1½ to 2 inches thick, cut in
   3 inch squares
Olive oil
Flour
1 medium onion, chopped fine

1 clove garlic, chopped fine
1½ cups water
2 tablespoons steak sauce
Louisiana Hot Sauce
1½ cups claret wine
Salt

Among the meats that may be used for this recipe are: sirloin, round, T-bone, chuck, loin tip, etc. If round steak is used, it will have to cook a little longer than the choicer cuts.

Cover bottom of skillet with olive oil and sear steak squares on all sides. Remove from skillet and place in baking pan. Put about three to four tablespoons of flour in the fat left in the skillet, turning the fire down so that it will cook slowly. Stir the flour constantly and if the mixture of fat and flour is too dry, add some more olive oil. Cook and stir until mixture is a rich brown. Add onions and garlic, stirring all the while, and then pour in 1½ cups of water. Stir this until it starts to form a thick gravy. Add steak sauce and Louisiana Hot Sauce to taste. Add more water if necessary to prevent burning when you are bringing it to a boil. Add wine and salt to taste and pour mixture over steak squares. Bake at 400 degrees for 30-45 minutes, basting frequently. Add water if needed. Serves 4 to 6.

"Me, I say cookin' is fun. An' here's four of us what done agree with me,
I garontee!"

BARBECUED ROAST OF BEEF

10 to 15 pound round heavy
  beef roast
6 to 8 green onions
  (shallots)
6 to 8 cloves garlic

6 to 8 green hot peppers
  (cayenne)
2 cups sauterne wine
Red ground cayenne pepper
Salt

Start fire in covered barbecue pit, using charcoal—not briquettes. Have fire going for about thirty minutes before meat is placed on it, then keep a slow fire going by adding charcoal when needed and also an occasional stick of wet hickory or pecan wood.

Puncture holes in the roast so you can put a clove of garlic, a green onion and a hot pepper in each hole. Rub salt and red ground pepper into the meat on all sides. Put enough olive oil in bottom of large baking pan to cover bottom well. Place roast in pan and put pan on barbecue fire. Close lid on the pit and let roast sear, turning to get all sides. (With a round roast, it is difficult to sear more than two sides). As soon as the roast is seared, pour wine into pan, not on the roast. Baste meat frequently with its own juices and turn it often. Cook for about 6 to 8 hours on a slow fire. If fire blazes up, sprinkle a little water on it. However, if fire is properly kept and pit is kept closed most of the time, blazing should not be a problem. If any additional juice is needed, mix ½ wine and ½ water and add.

CORNED BEEF AND CABBAGE AU VIN

Corned beef (3 to 5 pounds)
1 large cabbage
4 large onions (whole)
4 cups sauterne wine

2 tablespoons Lea & Perrins
1 cayenne pepper or dash of
  Louisiana Hot Sauce
Salt

Cover corned beef with water. Add sauterne wine, Lea & Perrins and cayenne pepper. Boil until tender (about 2 or 3 hours).
Remove corned beef.
Cut cabbage into quarters and add to stock with whole onions. Boil until tender. Salt to taste. Serves 6 to 8.

"Cast you' eye on that Jean-Pierre Malbrough. He makin' a grab for somethin' to eat while the rest of us is watchin' the birdie."

ROAST BEEF

10 pound heavy beef rump roast
  (with big bone removed)
6 small green onions
  (shallots)
6 green hot peppers
6 cloves garlic

Red pepper
Salt
3 tablespoons olive oil
3 cups Claret wine
Water
1 cup coarsely chopped onions

Punch holes in roast and put a one-inch piece of onion, a garlic clove and a pepper in each hole, along with a little salt. Rub salt and red pepper all over the roast. Put olive oil in roaster on top of stove. When hot enough, sear all sides of roast in the olive oil. Pour 3 cups of wine and a little water in roaster and add chopped onions. Place covered roaster in 400 degree pre-heated oven, basting occasionally. Cook 2½ hours for roast with medium rare center—longer if well done meat is desired. Serves 8 to 10.

SHORT RIB SPAGHETTI DINNER

7 beef short ribs (about 5
  pounds untrimmed)
2 medium onions, sliced
2 teaspoons salt
½ teaspoon pepper
1 teaspoon whole allspice
4 small bay leaves
2 beef bouillon cubes
2 cups hot water

1 8 ounce package spaghetti
2 10 ounce packages frozen peas
1 15½ ounce can onions
Melted butter or margarine
Paprika
Grated parmesan cheese
2 tablespoons flour
1 teaspoon sugar

About 2½ hours before serving time heat large greased Dutch oven until very hot. Add ribs, fat side down, cook over medium heat until well browned, about 30 minutes. Lay sliced onions in fat around meat, cook a minute or so, or until browned. Add salt, pepper, 1 teaspoon sugar, allspice, bay leaves, bouillon cubes, 2 cups hot water. Simmer (covered) from 1½ to 2 hours until ribs are tender.

Cook spaghetti. Cook peas. Heat large serving platter. Warm canned onions and toss in 2 tablespoons melted butter. Drain spaghetti, heap in center of platter, put short ribs around edge, alternating spoonfuls of peas, onions and ribs. Sprinkle peas and onions with paprika. Sprinkle Parmesan cheese on spaghetti, if desired. Skim fat from liquid. Slowly stir in ½ cup cold water, blended with flour and 1 teaspoon sugar. Cook until thickened and pass as gravy. Serves 8.

"If you don' taste while you' cookin', how you gonna know it good? Anyway, me, I got my hungers up all the time."

BARBECUED PORK OR BEEF RIBS

Pork ribs and/or beef ribs
Salt
Red pepper
Basting sauce

Beer
Lea & Perrins Worcestershire
Water

Salt and pepper ribs, put on barbecue pit, fire should be kept low. Make basting sauce by mixing half beer and half water, 1 teaspoon or 2 dashes of Lea & Perrins to each bottle of beer. Make basting sauce as needed. Baste ribs and turn frequently, baste before and after turning.

Just before ribs are ready to come off, baste both sides twice with barbecue sauce (see recipe on Page 85). Remember, pork must be well done.

If you prefer crisp, dry barbecued ribs . . . just use basting sauce, eliminate final barbecue sauce.

On a rainy day, this same effect can nearly be reached in your oven by adding 2 or 3 drops of liquid smoke to the basting sauce.

PORK CHOPS WITH DRESSING

2 cups bread crumbs
2 eggs
1 cup Claret wine
¼ cup olive oil
1 large onion, juiced or grated
2 cloves garlic, juiced or
  pressed

½ small bay leaf broken into
  tiny pieces
2 tablespoons steak sauce
1½ teaspoons Louisiana Cayenne
  Hot Sauce
6 pork chops, ¾ inch thick
Salt & red ground cayenne pepper

Put bread crumbs in a mixing bowl. Into this beat eggs and add a cup of wine, then the olive oil. Add onion, garlic and bay leaf. Mix well. Then add steak sauce and Louisiana Hot Sauce and mix well again. This mixture should be juicy and not dry. Add wine if it seems too dry and bread crumbs if too wet. Salt to taste. Take a casserole large enough to lay pork chops in a single layer and deep enough to hold the above mixture. Grease the casserole with olive oil and pour the dressing in it. Smooth it out and lay salted, red peppered pork chops on top. Bake in oven at about 350 degrees until done. Serves six.

"Jus' look at them beautifuls! An' we done brought them up on our own place, right here in Denham Springs, too."

BROILED PORK CHOPS AU VIN

10 pork chops, ¾ inch thick
Salt
Red cayenne pepper
¼ cup olive oil
2 green onions
2 cloves garlic

2 cups Sauterne or Claret wine
1 cup water
1 tablespoon Worcestershire
1 teaspoon Louisiana Hot Sauce
Juice of half a lemon

Salt and red pepper both sides of pork chops. Cover bottom of baking pan with olive oil—a generous covering—and also rub oil on sides of pan. Place pork chops in baking pan and put in broiler. While chops are broiling, dice green onions and garlic very fine. Put in skillet with a little oil and saute until soft, not done. Put wine and water on sauteed onions and garlic. Add Worcestershire, hot sauce, ½ teaspoon salt and the juice of ½ lemon. Simmer. While onions are being sauteed, pork chops should be turned. When both sides are brown, take pork chops from broiler and pour the sauteed onion mixture over them. Put in oven at 350 or 400 degrees. Let them cook until the gravy is done. Serve the gravy over steamed rice or creamed potatoes. Serves 4 or 5.

OVEN PORK ROAST

1 - 8 to 10 pound center cut
   loin roast

Salt and pepper
Chopped green onion tops

Salt and pepper roast well and place on rack in roasting pan with 1 inch water in bottom of pan. Cover and cook in 400 degree oven until almost done (about 2½ hours). Baste occasionally, add more water if needed. Take cover from roaster and score fatty side of roast, pat green onion tops all over top and cook uncovered until browned.

"This ain' no fancy supermarket. But if you want it an' that Cajun ain' got it, he gonna git it for you, for sure."

BAKED PORK CHOPS WITH RICE & TOMATOES

6 1-inch pork chops
2 cups cooked rice
1 large tomato (fresh or canned)
1 large bell pepper

1 medium onion (sliced)
2 No. 3 cans tomatoes
Salt
Pepper

In large skillet brown the pork chops that have been seasoned with salt and pepper. Place in large baking dish so each pork chop will be on the bottom. Cut green pepper in rings—place one on each pork chop. With ice cream scoop or large spoon dip rice, pat until firm and place in bell pepper ring. Place slice of onion on each and top with tomato slice. Empty canned tomatoes in pan and chop or squeeze until all tomatoes are broken up fine. Season with salt and pepper and pour around pork chops. Cover and steam one hour in oven at 375 degrees.

This is pretty as well as good.   Serves 6.

SWEETBREADS VEAU AUX CHAMPIGNONS A LA PIERRE

4 pounds sweetbreads
3 tablespoons olive oil
½ cup flour

2½ medium onions

2 cloves garlic
2 cups water
2½ cups Beaujolais (or
    any dry red wine)
1 medium can mushrooms

Clean sweetbreads, making sure to remove any excess skin. Cut into chunks. Put three tablespoons olive oil in large pot (preferably iron) and place sweetbreads in cold oil. Brown sweetbreads over medium fire and remove them from the pot. Add flour to olive oil remaining in pot (if necessary, add a little more oil) and turn fire down low. Stir constantly until ingredients are thoroughly mixed. When the roux becomes dark, almost burnt looking, add chopped onions and chopped garlic. When these are browned, add water and wine. Return sweetbreads to the simmering pot. Turn fire up to medium heat and cook for ½ hour, then add mushrooms. Cook for another ½ hour. May be served with steamed rice. Serves 6 to 8.

You axe almos' any ex-GI what was in Australia during Worl' War Twice an' he gonna told you that of all his unfavorite meats, lamb or mutton is his unfavoritest.

To tell the trut', I don' t'ink dat Australian mutton was mutton a-tall. It was some kind of ol' mountain goat. Hooey! Did that stuff ever have an aroma, one you ain't never gonna forgot?

But this leg of lamb is different, I garontee! In the firs' place, it is young, tender lamb, not tough ol' mutton. An' most important, it is the way we cook this leg of lamb.

The wine and the mint is what make the difference. An' if you have any trouble gettin' that mint to stay on that lamb, jus' mix it up wit' the wine and Lea & Perrins and it gonna stick, good.

When you buy leg of lamb, be sure and get you' butcher to remove the leg glands for you.

An' when you serve this dish, even to an ex-GI, you gonna hear them raves.

BARBECUED HAM

8 to 10 lb. pre-cooked ham
3 cloves garlic
6 green onions

3 hot peppers (cayenne, chile
    cortillas, etc.)
Barbecue sauce

With sharp knife, score ham. Punch holes in ham with sharp knife. Space the holes so you will have about 6. In each hole stuff one piece green onion, ½ clove garlic, ½ hot pepper. Place ham in baking pan. Do not cover. Pour hot barbecue sauce (see Page 85 for recipe) over ham liberally, leaving at least 1 inch of barbecue sauce in bottom of pan. Place in oven (400 degrees) or in covered barbecue pit over slow fire and cook for about 1½ hours. Use charcoal, not briquettes, and add some hickory chips if barbecue pit is used.

ROAST LEG OF LAMB

1 leg of lamb
4 cups sauterne wine
3 tablespoons dry mint
1 tablespoon dry mustard
5 cloves garlic

6 green onions
6 pickled or fresh hot peppers
1 tablespoon Lea & Perrins
Salt
Red pepper

Wipe leg of lamb well with dry cloth. Using sharp knife, punch 6 holes in leg of lamb. In each hole place garlic clove, green onion and either pickled or fresh hot pepper. After this is done, salt leg of lamb well and pepper it with cayenne pepper. Pat 3 tablespoons of dry mint flakes on entire leg of lamb. Put enough olive oil in a baking pan to keep lamb from burning. Place the lamb in baking pan and put in 400 degree oven and sear the lamb on all sides. After the lamb is seared add 1 tablespoon of Lea & Perrins and 4 cups sauterne wine. Baste lamb frequently and if any additional juice is needed, add half wine and half water. Continue cooking at 400 degrees to your taste. Usual cooking time, about 2 hours.

"This is a little snack we done cook up one night at the Houston Press Club. Wasn' but twenty-two differen' dishes on the menu."

CHICKEN

CHICKEN JAMBALAYA

3 cups long grain rice
1 large fryer
6 medium size onions (chopped)
1 clove garlic
    (finely chopped)
1 tablespoon bell pepper
    (chopped small)

1 tablespoon celery (chopped
    small)
½ pound hot smoked sausage, if
    desired
Salt
Black pepper
Cayenne pepper
1 cup cooking oil

Cut up chicken, wash and season with salt and both peppers. Fry until golden brown in cooking oil over hot fire. Lower heat and add all chopped seasoning except garlic. Cook until all seasoning is clear or onions, bell pepper and celery are tender. Here's where you may add the hot sausage. I think this makes a better jambalaya. Add rice, salt and pepper to chicken and seasoning. Cook slowly for about 15 minutes over low heat, stirring often. Add 4 cups water and chopped garlic, stir and cover. Do not stir anymore. Simmer over low flame for about 1 hour, or until rice is done. Keep covered.

Variations: This same recipe may be used with pork, duck, squirrel, rabbit, sausage or beef. Serves 8, an' good!

"Couple ol' Cajuns sometime spend a whole afternoon like this——seein' who can lie the bes'!"

CHICKEN A LA JUSTIN

2 fryers
4 cups chopped dry onions
1 cup chopped shallots, or green onions
1 cup chopped bell pepper
1 cup chopped celery
2 cups chopped parsley (or 1 cup
   dried parsley)
1 small can pimento

Salt
Red pepper (Cayenne
   preferably)
Black pepper
Olive oil
4 cups sauterne wine
2 tablespoons Lea & Perrins
Dash of Louisiana Hot Sauce

Cut chicken as if to fry. Season with black pepper, red pepper and salt. Pour olive oil in bottom of baking pan. Put chicken in pan. Sprinkle over the chopped onions, bell pepper, celery and parsley. Cut pimento in strips and place on chicken. Mix wine, Lea & Perrins and dash of hot sauce. Pour over chicken and bake, uncovered, at 375 degrees until chicken is browned. Approximately 1½ to 2 hours. Baste frequently. Add water if needed. Serves 4 to 6.

POULET AU GRATIN A LA CASTILLE

2 tablespoons olive oil
1 two pound fryer
2 medium sized onions
4 medium cloves garlic
¼ cup water

1 can cream of mushroom soup
1 cup sauterne wine
Medium sized can mushrooms
¼ pound grated Romano cheese

Cover bottom of skillet with olive oil. Place cut up chicken in cold olive oil. Brown chicken until almost done. Remove chicken. In same skillet and oil, place chopped onions and garlic and brown them. When brown, add ¼ cup wine. Put chicken back into skillet and simmer fifteen minutes. Then place contents of skillet into a casserole. Pour over chicken in casserole mushroom soup and then add ¾ cup wine. Add can of mushrooms and sprinkle grated cheese on top. Bake until chicken is tender (about 45 minutes). Serves 6.

"Sara an' me, we gonna take time out from cookin' to see if maybe the drinkin' wine done gone bad or somethin'."

PEACH BRANDY CHICKEN

1 broiler——2½ pound
1 No. 1 can light syrup peaches,
   yellow—halves (drained)
½ cooking apple, sliced
2 teaspoons salt
1 teaspoon Accent
½ teaspoon black pepper

½ teaspoon seasoning salt
2 tablespoons olive oil
⅓ cup claret wine
1 cup celery, mostly leaves and
   a little stalk, chopped fine
⅓ cup brandy

Cut broiler in half, wash and pat dry. Use seasoning salt, Accent, and pepper. Put olive oil in iron pot, brown chicken golden brown. With ribs down add celery and apple. Cook slowly, covered, for 30 minutes. Turn chicken, ribs up, pour claret wine, cover and cook 15 minutes. Add peaches pit side up and ⅓ cup brandy, pouring some in each peach half and in rib side of chicken. Cover and heat. Take fork and mash gravy with care to get out all lumps, bring to boil when ready to serve chicken. Serves 2-4.

BROILED CHICKEN

Salt
Red ground pepper
3 frying or broiling chickens,
   halved

½ cup olive oil
1 cup sauterne wine
  (more if needed)

Rub salt and red pepper well into chicken. Cover bottom of baking pan with olive oil. Then pour in wine, mixing it with the olive oil as much as possible. Wet each side of chicken with this mixture and place the halves in the pan. Put under broiler, basting frequently till done. Serves 6.

BARBECUED CHICKEN

Halves of broiler or fryer
   chickens

Basting sauce
Barbecue sauce

Place chicken halves on low charcoal fire, turn frequently and baste both sides before and after turning with basting sauce on Page 25. When chickens are done, finish off with two bastings of barbecue sauce on Page 85. Put in pan and pour any remaining barbecue sauce over them.

"Me, I got a frien'. Pete his front name, Fountain his behin' name."

CHICKEN-ANDOUILLE GUMBO A LA ROSINA

1 large stewing chicken
*1 pound andouille—sliced in ¼ inch
   slices (gumbo sausage)
6 large white or yellow onions,
   chopped
1 small bunch green onions,
   cut fine
1 small bell pepper, chopped
1 tablespoon chopped celery

1 tablespoon finely chopped
   parsley
1 clove garlic, chopped
Salt, black pepper and red
   cayenne pepper
¾ cup all-purpose flour
   (for roux)
1 cup cooking oil
6 cups hot water

Cut up chicken, wash and season with salt and pepper. Heat 1 cup oil in heavy skillet and fry chicken until brown. Remove chicken and put aside. Pour remaining oil into large heavy pot for making roux without tomatoes on Page 1.

After roux is made, lower heat and add all chopped ingredients, except green onions, garlic, and parsley. Cover and simmer until onions are clear, stirring occasionally.

Add sliced andouille and chicken to roux mixture, cover and let simmer about ½ hour. Stir often during this process. Keep heat low through this point.

Add water, garlic, parsley and green onions. You may increase heat until mixture begins to boil. Now lower heat to simmer, cover and cook 1½ to 2 hours or until chicken is tender.

This has a lot of liquid and is served on rice, over which ¼ teaspoon filé has been sprinkled. It's even better next day.
Variations:

This same recipe may be used for duck, rabbit, squirrel. In making seafood gumbo, such as shrimp, crab or oysters, the only exception, of course, is that there will be no frying of the particular seafood being used.

*You are probably wondering what andouille is. Well, I'm gonna tell you. It is a special sausage we French people make, of chopped pork and seasoned especially for use in gumbo. It is pronounced "ohn-dewey."

Ask your butcher to get you some. You'll love it.

If for some reason, your butcher was not educate in south Louisiana, an' he don' know somethin' about this andouille, forgot about it—an' him. You gonna have damn good gumbo anyhow.

Filé, what make you' gumbo so good and thick, ain' either a file or a filet. It jus' what it said, tilé.

An' it's made from the leaves of a sassafras tree. It's in powdered form and you can get it mos' any good grocery store.

Remember what I done tol' you. Don' put filé in the gumbo while it's cookin'. You don' add the filé to the gumbo in the pot. Jus' sprinkle a little on the gumbo when you dish it up.

An' this gumbo is another of them Cajun dishes what tastes even better warmed over the nex' day, if they any lef', which I doubt.

SEAFOOD

SHRIMP AND OYSTER GUMBO WITH FILÉ

1½ cups sifted flour
1 small can tomato sauce
1 small can tomato paste
2 large onions, chopped fine
1 large clove garlic, chopped fine
1 medium bell pepper, chopped fine
1 pint fresh oysters
1 to 2 pounds peeled shrimp

Fresh hot pepper or
   Louisiana Hot Sauce
Salt
4 cups sauterne wine
Olive oil
2 tablespoons Lea & Perrins
Water

Use pot that will hold 6 quarts. Make a roux with tomato sauce and paste, (see page 1). Add chopped onions and garlic, bell pepper. Keep stirring so that mixture will not burn. Add wine mixed with equal parts of water. This mixture should be thicker than a soup and additional water should be added to get this consistency. Add hot pepper or 2 teaspoons of Louisiana Hot Sauce and Lea & Perrins. Bring this to a boil, add shrimp and oysters. Cook on a slow fire for about 2 hours. This should serve from 8 to 12 persons.

If there is any left over, refrigerate or freeze remainder. The left-overs often taste better than when first served.

Filé is a powder made from the leaves of a sassafras tree. You can buy filé in 'mos' any grocery store. It is what makes your gumbo thick enough after it has been cooked. Don't put filé in gumbo until it has cooked. Actually, you should put it in the gumbo when you serve it with the rice. Serve with steamed rice. Serves 8.

For crab gumbo substitute crab bodies and claws. You may also use leftover duck. It makes a wonderful gumbo, too.

Jus' peal an' eat them shrimp. You don' need no sauce, 'cause they delicious jus' as they is. While they is cookin', pick one up ever' now an' then an' taste it to see if it done. I can't never wait more'n about five or four minutes to try this, myself.

BOILED SHRIMP IN SHELL

4 quarts water (enough to cover
   shrimp)
8 lemons, quartered
3 large onions, quartered
2 cloves garlic, coarsely
   chopped
1 stalk celery, coarsely chopped

3 cups sauterne wine
2 tablespoons Lea & Perrins
   Worcestershire
Salt
2 tablespoons ground cayenne
   pepper
5 pounds shrimp, raw

Put water in a pot large enough to hold shrimp and all the seasoning, and place it on a hot fire. Drop into the water the lemons, onions, garlic and celery. Add wine and Worcestershire. Add salt until fluid is too salty for your taste. Bring to a boil and then add the shrimp. Cook from 20 to 35 minutes depending on the size of the shrimp. Watch the shrimp and when the hull stands away from the meat, they are done. Another way to tell is that they usually float. (The best way to determine whether the shrimp are done is to taste them after 15 or 20 minutes of boiling.)

Pour juice off shrimp and let them steam for about 15 minutes. Then place on a large tray and cool. Serves 4 to 6.

VARIATION: Substitute 2 or 3 dozen crabs for shrimp. Add more salt since crabs and other shell fish require more salt than does shrimp.

DRESSING FOR BOILED SHRIMP

4 heaping tablespoons mayonnaise
1 large bottle (16 ounce) catsup
2 tablespoons olive oil
2 teaspoons Louisiana Hot Sauce
1 teaspoon salt

1 tablespoon Lea & Perrins
   Worcestershire
Juice of 1 whole lemon
1 level tablespoon prepared
   creamed style horse radish

Place mayonnaise in bowl, add olive oil slowly, beating constantly, with fork. Beat mayonnaise back to original firmness. Add Louisiana hot sauce, then add catsup, beating all the while. Add salt and Lea & Perrins. Squeeze lemon into catsup bottle, getting remains of catsup, pour into mixture, add horse radish, cover and chill for about 30 minutes. Beat just before serving. Additional horse radish may be added to individual serving, if desired.

Them broiled shrimp is a little bit tricky. Don' you broil them too long, an' not too fast, an' they will be good, I garontee.

One time I slip up a little an' broil them too long. They did not taste too good, but they sure made nice new half-soles for my shoes!

SHRIMP A LA CREOLE

1 pound raw shrimp (deveined)
½ cup onion, chopped
1 small clove garlic, minced
½ cup celery, chopped
½ cup parsley, chopped
⅓ cup bell (sweet) pepper, chopped
3 tablespoons olive oil
2 cups water

2 cups tomatoes
1 cup tomato puree (sauce)
½ teaspoon Lea & Perrins
   Worcestershire
½ teaspoon Louisiana Hot Sauce
   (cayenne)
1 teaspoon salt
3 cups cooked rice

Saute onion, celery, parsley and bell pepper until tender. Add water, tomatoes, tomato puree and garlic. Simmer 5 minutes, add Lea & Perrins, Louisiana Hot Sauce and salt.

Cook mixture for 30 minutes. Add shrimp and cook for 30 more minutes, or until shrimp are done and mixture is thick.

Serve over rice—4 portions.

BROILED SHRIMP A LA JUSTIN

¼ cup olive oil
1 stick butter or oleo
2 teaspoons Worcestershire
1 teaspoon Louisiana Red Hot Sauce

3 pounds raw peeled shrimp
Salt
Red ground cayenne pepper
1 cup sauterne wine

Put olive oil in bottom of baking pan and chip butter into it. Place in oven until butter is melted. Then take pan out and add Worcestershire and hot sauce. Mix well. Put shrimp in single layer into the mixture and salt and red pepper them. Pour wine into pan, using approximately 1 cup or as much as is needed to half cover the shrimp. Place in preheated 350 degree oven for 20 minutes. Then place in broiler until shrimp begin to brown. Baste frequently.

If you like to eat jus' a little bit, I think this is the mos' delicious fried shrimp recipe I done ever taste.

If you can possibly marinate them shrimp about 12 hours, or maybe overnight, they gonna soak up all that juices an' taste even better.

FRENCH FRIED SHRIMP

4 eggs
Milk
1 cup Parmesan cheese
2 large onions
1 clove garlic
1 cup sauterne wine

1 bell pepper
1 tablespoon Lea & Perrins
    Worcestershire
1 teaspoon hot sauce (Louisiana)
Pancake flour
3 lbs. shrimp (de-veined)
Salt

Slice onions, garlic, bell (sweet) pepper and blend in blender. Place in large bowl over shrimp. Beat 4 eggs, adding sauterne wine slowly while beating. Pour this over shrimp, adding Lea & Perrins and hot sauce. Add in the cheese. Stir this mixture well. Add milk to cover shrimp. Stir until milk mixes well. Salt to taste. Marinate overnight.

Place pancake flour (as much as needed) in brown paper sack, adding a little salt. Drain shrimp a few at a time and shake in pancake flour. Fry in deep fat. Serves 4 to 6.

CRAWFISH STEW

3 pounds crawfish tails
    (cleaned and de-veined)
4 medium onions (chopped)
½ cup chopped bell pepper
½ cup chopped celery
1 cup parsley, chopped (½ cup dried
    parsley)

1 clove garlic (finely chopped)
1 cup flour
½ cup olive oil
Salt
Black pepper
Red pepper

Use an iron pot, if possible. Heat cooking oil, add flour and brown to a dark brown over a low fire. Be certain to keep stirring this mixture constantly. If the phone rings, don't answer.

Add chopped seasoning, simmer over low heat about 1 hour.

Season crawfish tails with salt, black and red pepper and add to above sauce mixture. Cover and simmer together for about one-half hour. Keep the heat low. Add 3 cups of water, cover and continue to simmer over low heat for about 1 more hour. Serve over rice. Serves 6 to 8.

When you stick a fork in this fish and it come out with a little bits of fish clingin' to it this is did, for sure. It become flaky when it is did.

An' that's when you start snappin' at each other when you eat it. That's why they name it red snapper, I guess.

You mus' watch this fish broilin' quite a bit, an' baste it with them juices, which are jus' wondermous. I even know me some people what t'row them fishes away an' just sop up the juice.

Hoo, boy! What a big lie that was!

Oh, yes, if you use froze fish, be dam' sure to thaw it plumb out before you cooks it. An' that's a order!

BROILED FLOUNDER

1 bunch green onions
1 large clove garlic
Olive oil
Salt

Red pepper (Cayenne)
4 medium sized dressed flounder
2 cups sauterne wine

Cover the bottom of a sauce pan with olive oil. Put finely diced onions and garlic in it and cook until soft. While this is being done, cover the bottom of a large baking pan or some kind of ovenware with olive oil about ⅛ of an inch deep. Salt and pepper the flounder and place in the pan. Pour wine into pan, being careful not to wash the salt and pepper off the fish. Spread softened onions and garlic over the flounder. Broil until done. (It might be well to bake the fish in a 350 degree oven for about 10 or 15 minutes before putting it under the broiler.) Serves 4 to 6, depending on how flounder hungry you are. Makes you slap your wife if she reach for that last little piece of flounder.

BAKED RED SNAPPER

2½ cups chopped green onions
1 leaf chopped celery
2 13 ounce cans mushrooms, stems and pieces
Olive oil for sauteeing
¼ cup olive oil
Salt
Red ground cayenne pepper

1 large red snapper—6 to 10 pounds
2 tablespoons dried parsley flakes
3 cups sauterne wine
4 dashes wine vinegar
1 tablespoon Lea & Perrins Worcestershire

Saute onions, celery and mushrooms in a frying pan in a little olive oil.
Pour olive oil in baking pan. Salt and red pepper the fish to taste and place it in the pan. Spread sauteed onions, celery and mushrooms over the fish. Now sprinkle the parsley on top of the other ingredients. Rinse frying pan (used for sauteeing) with the wine and pour over fish. Bake at 375 degrees, basting occasionally, until fish is cooked. Serves 8 to 10.

"Hoo, boy! How can anything taste so good look so bad? Huh?"

CATFISH COURTBOUILLON (COO-BEE-YON)

1 large catfish (3 to 6 pounds)
8 medium onions (chopped)
4 cups green onions (chopped)
1 cup celery (chopped)
½ cup chopped bell pepper
1 clove garlic, chopped fine

½ cup parsley, finely chopped
  (using dried parsley use ¼ cup)
1 cup flour
½ cup olive oil
Salt and pepper (black & cayenne
  pepper)
2 Cups water

Heat cooking oil. Add flour and brown. Add chopped seasoning. Simmer 1 hour. Cut up fish in large pieces. Season with salt and both peppers. Add to the above sauce. Add water. Cover and cook over low heat about 1 hour. Serve over rice. Serves 6 to 8.

TURTLE ETOUFFEE

Olive oil
10 pounds turtle meat (cleaned)
8 large onions (chopped well)
3 bell pepper (chopped well)
1 clove garlic (finely chopped)

Juice of one-half lemon
1 cup of parsley,(chopped)
  (if using dried parsley use ½
  cup)
Salt and pepper
1 tablespoon Lea & Perrins
  Worcestershire

Wash and drain turtle meat. Salt and pepper and brown in olive oil. Put in heavy pot and add all other ingredients. Cook on low heat from 6 to 8 hours, until turtle meat is tender. Serve with rice.

Note: The only juice in the Turtle Etouffee is the natural juice of the vegetable ingredients. Do not add water, wine or any other juice.

"Until I gone and los' me some weights, you ain' gonna got me in that pirogue some at all!"

GAME

BAKED GOOSE

1 domestic or wild goose
1 cup flour
½ to ¾ cup olive oil
2 large onions (chopped)
2 cloves garlic (minced)
1 can cream mushroom soup
3 cups sauterne wine
Red ground cayenne pepper
Salt

Vinegar
1 lemon, juice of
1 small bay leaf
1 tablespoon Lea & Perrins
  Worcestershire
1 turnip, peeled whole
3 cups water
½ cup parsley

If the goose is wild, marinate in ¼ vinegar and ¾ water to cover goose for 4 to 12 hours. If goose is domestic, marinate in this type mixture 1 to 3 hours. Remove goose from mixture and wash real well with cold water. Drain well. Salt and pepper (with red cayenne) the goose. Place turnip inside goose. Brown flour slowly, over low fire, in olive oil in roaster until brown, add onions, parsley. Stir for 2 or 3 minutes. Add water, garlic, wine, mushroom soup, lemon juice, Lea & Perrins, bay leaf (on toothpicks to be removed after 1 hour of cooking). Place goose on rack and place in roaster, cover and baste occasionally. Add water if necessary. Add salt and pepper to gravy if needed. Cook in 375 degree oven 2 hours, removing cover to brown if needed.

"Me, I don' cook all the time. Sometime I gotta work at bein' a safety engineer, too."

BROILED QUAIL

6 quail
Salt
Red ground cayenne pepper

Olive oil
½ cup sauterne wine
½ lemon

Split dressed birds down the back. Salt and red pepper them, rubbing seasonings well into birds. Cover bottom of broiling pan with olive oil, about ⅛ inch deep and rub sides of pan with oil also. Add ½ cup sauterne. Place birds in pan and place 3 inches away from preheated broiler for 8 to 10 minutes, basting frequently. Turn and broil on other side for same amount of time, basting again. Squeeze lemon over quail about 5 minutes before removing from broiler. Serve on buttered toast, surrounded by sauteed mushrooms. Serves 4 to 6.

PHEASANT AU VIN

2 large pheasants, whole
Water
Wine vinegar
Salt
Olive oil

Red ground cayenne pepper
2 8-ounce cans cream of mush-
   room soup
1 bay leaf
2 cups sauterne wine

Wash birds well and let them drain. Marinate for about an hour in a mixture of water, wine vinegar and salt. Remove, rinse lightly and drain. Cover bottom of baking pan with olive oil. Place pheasants in baking pan after salting and red peppering them well, rubbing the seasonings into the birds. Add cream of mushroom soup and bay leaf. Cover pan and place in preheated slow oven (200 degrees) for 30 minutes. Add wine and then cook for about 2 more hours or until meat is done. Baste about every 15 to 20 minutes. The last few minutes of baking may be done with the cover off for browning. Serves 4 to 6.

This recipe works jus' fine with any fowl that cooks dry.

"Alma Picou, she say she catch them catfish if me, I'll cook them. An'
I will, too!"

VENISON SAUCE PIQUANTE

4 pounds round of venison, cut
   in 2 inch cubes
8 medium size onions, chopped
2 bunches green onions, chopped
1 large bell pepper, chopped
1 cup chopped celery
2 - 8 ounce cans tomato sauce
1 cup olive oil

2 cloves garlic, chopped
2 tablespoons Worcestershire sauce
Juice of 2 lemons
¾ cup bacon drippings
1 cup all purpose flour (for roux)
Salt, black pepper & red cayenne
   pepper
6 cups water

Wash venison, season with salt and pepper, and fry in bacon drippings, until brown. Remove from fat and set aside. Using olive oil and flour, make a roux with tomato sauce and paste (see directions on Page 1).

Add all chopped seasoning, except garlic, cover and simmer on low heat for about 1 hour. Add venison to roux and chopped seasoning mixture. Simmer for 30 minutes, covered.

Add water and garlic, cover and let cook slowly for about 2 hours.

Serve over rice or spaghetti.

(For Turtle Sauce Piquante, merely substitute 5 pounds of boned, washed turtle meat for venison. Lots of us Cajuns like Turtle Sauce Piquante best.)

VENISON ROAST

6 to 8 pound venison roast
Vinegar
Water
Salt
Red ground cayenne pepper
Olive oil

2 cups chopped onion
2 cloves garlic
2 cups claret wine
1 small bay leaf
2 tablespoons Lea & Perrins
   Worcestershire

Marinate venison in strong vinegar-water solution for about 2 hours. Remove and rinse well. Dry meat off. Rub salt and red pepper into meat. Cover bottom of baking pan with olive oil. Place roast in pan and sear the meat on top of stove. Add onions and garlic (chopped large), then the wine and 2 cups of water. Add bay leaf and Worcestershire. Place pan, covered, in semi-slow oven, about 300 to 350 degrees. Cook until done, basting frequently. Serves 6.

"It don' make t'ings taste more better, but sometime me, I jus' gotta dress the part, too."

DOVES OR QUAIL IN WINE SAUCE   (Very Good)

15 doves or quail
Salt & pepper to taste
2 cups of flour
1½ cups cooking oil
2 large onions, chopped very
   fine

Celery to equal the same amount
   as onions, also chopped very fine
2 cups sauterne wine
2 cups water
3 bay leaves
½ stick butter, cut in squares

Salt & pepper doves or quail, dust with flour and brown in cooking oil. Place doves in large ovenware casserole, sprinkle onions and celery over the game. Pour wine and water over this. Dot with butter and stick bay leaves with toothpicks, so they can be readily found. Place bay leaves, with toothpicks, in the game. Cover casserole tightly and bake at 375 degrees, until onions and celery are almost clear, approximately 2 hours. Baste occasionally. This gravy is very good over rice.

BROILED SQUIRREL

3 squirrels with head removed
¼ cup olive oil
1 cup claret or sauterne wine

Salt
Vinegar & water
Red ground pepper

Marinate squirrel in mixture of vinegar & water, ¼ vinegar to ¾ water, a minimum of 3 hours, preferably longer, up to 24 hours.

After marinating, wash squirrels with cold water. Salt and pepper. Grease pan with some of the olive oil, pour the rest over squirrels after they are placed in pan. Add wine. Baste often.

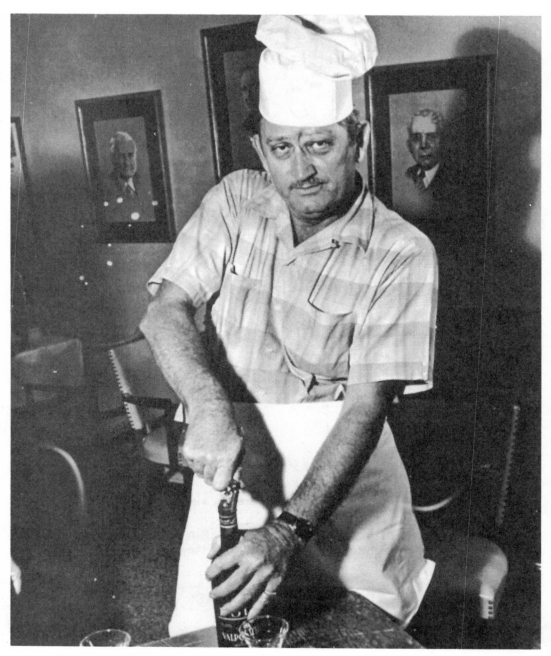

"What did you said? Cook without wine? C'mon now, how you gonna did that, huh?"

BARBECUED DUCK
(Wild or Domestic)

3 to 6 ducks
1 cup vinegar
Sauterne wine
Water
Olive oil

Small onions
Small potatoes or turnips
Garlic pods
Salt
Cayenne pepper

Wash duck carcasses carefully, then place in deep pan and cover with vinegar and half and half mixture of wine and water. Let ducks soak 2 hours, then drain. Insert in each duck 1 small onion, 1 small potato or turnip, ½ small clove of garlic. Place ¼ inch olive oil in bottom of deep pan. Heat over charcoal fire in hooded barbecue pit. Then add ducks, after salt and cayenne pepper have been sprinkled generously on ducks. Sear ducks on all sides in olive oil, turning, add 1½ cups wine in bottom of pan. Baste well. In 10 minutes add ½ cup water and ½ cup wine. Baste frequently until ducks are done. Add more wine and water mixture, if needed.

"That ol' Mississippi is a plumb good place for me to do my contemplate', I garontee!"

VEGETABLES

DIRTY RICE

2 pounds lean ground beef
2 pounds lean ground pork
1 pound chicken giblets (ground)
1 cup yellow onions (diced)
1 cup diced shallots (green onions)
½ cup diced bell (sweet) peppers
¼ cup garlic (preferably ground)

¼ cup parsley (cut up fine)
4 bay leaves
1 teaspoon black pepper
2 cans cream of mushroom soup
2 cups celery (cut up fine)
3 tablespoons Lea & Perrins Sauce
½ pound margarine or butter
Salt

With about 2 cups of water, mix all meats together in a heavy pot, on a medium hot burner. Add all the above seasoning ingredients except mushroom soup at the start of cooking. Cook medium speed approximately 4 hours. Stir often. Then add the cream of mushroom soup. Continue cooking for 30 minutes. Boil 2 pounds long grain rice (see recipe on Page 65). Let rice cook completely. After rice has cooked, mix with the meat ingredients thoroughly. Allow to steam or cook on a low heat for approximately 30 minutes before serving. Serves 10.

Sometimes, when I'm real hongry——which is mos' of the time——I puts a slice of boiled ham on top of them red beans an' rice. Hoo, boy! That's plumb good!

RICE (long grain)

Place as much rice as you need in a heavy pan. Cover with water until the water is first joint deep above the level of the rice. Use the middle finger to measure, since the first joint of the middle finger is the same length in every normal-sized adult, believe it or not! Add salt to taste, usually about two teaspoonsful. Place over hottest flame and let it come to rapid boil. Boil in this fashion until you can't see any water bubbling in the holes which will appear in the surface. Then, turn heat to simmer and simmer for 30-40 minutes, with pan lid on. Don't even peek at it until you're ready to serve it. Above all, don't panic. If you follow this carefully, you won't burn a damn t'ing, I garontee!

DRIED RED BEANS

1 pound red kidney beans
2 large onions
2 cloves garlic
1 green hot pepper (or 1½ tea-
    spoon Louisiana Hot Sauce)
Claret wine

Water
Olive oil
¼ pound ham or salt shoulder or
    pickled shoulder of pork
Salt

Wash beans well, getting all the grit and rocks out of them. Place in an earthenware or glass bowl. Chop up onions, garlic and pepper and add them to the beans. If you don't have a hot pepper, add Louisiana Hot Sauce. Pour a mixture of one half wine and one half water over the beans so that they are covered by an inch or more of liquid. Let these beans soak or marinate overnight. You may have to add 1 cup wine and 1 cup water to them before you go to bed or before you put them on in the morning. The next morning, cover the bottom of a heavy pot (preferably iron) with about ½ cup olive oil. Add meat that you have decided to use and heat. Pour beans and the mixture in which they have marinated into pot. Add water if it is necessary. Bring to a good boil, then turn fire down and cook slowly for several hours until done. Add salt just before you think the beans are done and let it cook into the beans. Serve these beans over steamed rice. Serves 4 to 6. (This recipe may be applied to white beans or dried peas, using sauterne wine in place of claret.)

"Me and them onion, we got us a——how-you-call it——affinity. Me, I ain' shed my firs' tear, 'til yet."

OKRA GUMBO

When making Okra Gumbo, you may use chicken or any of the variations, mentioned in Nos. 1 and 2 for Chicken Andouille Gumbo a La Rosina, Page 39.

Follow same directions, using same ingredients, but add 2 cups chopped okra and 2 large, peeled fresh tomatoes or 1 can No. 3 tomatoes.

To add these 2 ingredients, grease a heavy skillet (preferably aluminum), saute chopped okra, stirring often, for about 20 minutes, then add tomatoes and, while stirring, mash tomatoes, so that they mix well with okra.

You may add these ingredients just before adding the water, garlic, parsley and green onions, as in Chicken Andouille Gumbo.

It is not necessary to use tomatoes. You may use only okra, if you prefer.

CUT OKRA AND TOMATOES AU VIN

2 tablespoons olive oil
6 slices thick bacon,
　cubed
2 medium onions chopped
　fine
1 clove garlic, minced
2 pounds fresh cut okra

4 medium tomatoes cut into 6
　or 8 pieces each
1 cup sauterne wine
1 or 2 teaspoons Louisiana Hot
　Sauce
1 tablespoon Lea & Perrins
Salt

Put olive oil in a skillet large enough so that mixture can be stirred. Add cubed bacon, onions and minced garlic. Saute this for about ten minutes. Add okra and tomatoes. Pour wine over this and add hot sauce and Lea & Perrins. Salt to taste. Cook until okra is tender and has lost green taste. Serves 8.

This is one of them dishes you can cook when you don' feel like cookin' much at all. When you don' feel like dirtyin' up a whole lot of pots, an' you don' feel like watchin' anything real close, cook this.

Oh, yes, an' befo' I forgot to tol' you this, when I say cube the sausage or ham, I don' mean little bitty pieces, none either. I mean maybe two-inch squares, so you' gonna feel like you' eatin' somethin'.

BOILED OKRA

2 pounds fresh young okra
½ cup olive oil
2 cups sauterne wine

1 cup water
2 teaspoons Louisiana Hot Sauce
2 teaspoons salt

Wash okra well. Put olive oil in pot, then add the okra. Pour wine and water over it and add Louisiana Hot Sauce and salt. Bring to a good boil and then turn fire down and cook slowly until okra is tender.

One thing to remember, leave a small portion of stem on okra. This keeps it from gettin' slickery. Serves 8.

BOILED CABBAGE DINNER

Olive oil
1 cabbage, medium sized,
    quartered
4 to 6 large onions, peeled,
    whole
4 to 6 medium Irish potatoes,
    peeled, whole

4 to 6 carrots, peeled, whole
3 cups sauterne wine
3 cups water
Louisiana Hot Sauce
Salt
1½ to 2 pounds smoked pork
    sausage or cubed ham

Use a pot large enough to hold all of the vegetables and meat. Cover bottom of pot with olive oil, at least ¼ cup and maybe a little more. Put cabbage into pot. Then add the onions, potatoes and carrots. Next add wine and water. After adding Louisiana Hot Sauce and salt to taste, bring to a boil. Then add meat. Add more water if necessary. Cook until meat and potatoes are done. This can be used as a full meal and should serve from 4 to 6.

You gonna make you'self some new frien's with this recipe, I garontee! When they axe you what is this wondermous aroma and this marvelmous taste, you can tell them it smell that way and taste that way because you use three different kinds of cheese, not jus' one. This is what really gives it a unusual flavor. Only maybe you don' want to told them you' secret some at all. In that case, jus' smile real sweetlike an' tell them it ain' none of they dam' business how you did that.

In my travels——an' I is a much-traveled Cajun, I garontee——I have done eat mos' every kind cookin' they is. But, to tol' the trut', I would rather eat at Marie O'Neill's house than jus' about any place I can thought of.

An' I would jus' about rather eat this cabbage roll than anythin' I can thought of right at this moment, here.

You ain' gonna believe cabbage an' meat roll together like this could taste so good as this do, but it do.

EGGPLANTS

3 medium eggplants
Olive oil
½ teaspoon salt
1 cup white bread crumbs
1 cup Italian style bread
  crumbs
½ cup Romano cheese
2 cups American cheese, grated

½ pound mild Swiss cheese,
  slices
4 eggs
½ cup sauterne wine
4 small onions
2 cloves garlic
2 teaspoons Louisiana Hot Sauce
1 tablespoon Lea & Perrins

Peel and chop eggplants and soak about 30 minutes in salt water. Drain. Put 2 tablespoons olive oil in bottom of pan and 2 cups water. Parboil eggplants until they can be mashed with a fork. Mash and beat. Add salt, two types of bread crumbs, Romano cheese. Fold together. Beat eggs in sauterne wine. Puree onions and garlic. Mix these two ingredients with the eggs well beaten, then add hot sauce and Lea & Perrins. Add to eggplant mixture. Mix well. Prepare large casserole with 3½ tablespoons olive oil in bottom, put about a 1-inch layer of eggplant mixture in the casserole, then a thick layer of grated American cheese. Add another layer of eggplant, then another thick layer of American cheese. Cover casserole with thin slices of mild Swiss cheese, bake until done. Serves 6 to 8.

CABBAGE ROLL A LA MARIE

1 pound ground meat
1 cup raw rice
1 egg
Onion
Garlic

Pepper
1 can tomato sauce or ½ cup
  ketchup
¼ cup claret wine
1 head cabbage

Mix all ingredients except cabbage together in a bowl. Separate cabbage into leaves, trimming away all the tough part of the stem of each leaf. Place leaves in a pan of water to tenderize. When soft, place a generous tablespoon of the meat-rice mixture into each cabbage leaf and roll edges of leaf around it. The roll may be secured by toothpick. Put the rolls into a sauce pan. Dilute a can of tomato sauce and pour the liquid over the rolls. Cook from 30 to 40 minutes. Serves 4 to 6.

If you can't get them fresh beans, bought you'self some froze ones.

But when you cook them, jus' throw away them instructs on the outside package.

What you do with them is toss them in the pot wit' all them other ingredients, like the recipe done tol' you, and cook them until they are tender. Then you salt them to you' taste.

SNAP OR STRING BEANS AU VIN

2 pounds fresh snap beans
½ cup olive oil
2 slices thick bacon, cubed
2 medium sized chopped onions
1 small clove garlic, chopped

2 or 3 cups sauterne wine
1 tablespoon Lea & Perrins
Louisiana Hot Sauce (cayenne)
Salt
Water, if needed

Snap and string the beans. Pour olive oil into pot big enough to hold all the beans with ease (preferably an iron pot). Put bacon in olive oil and fry until soft, not brown. Add beans, onions, garlic and wine. Add Lea and Perrins and season with Louisiana Hot Sauce to taste, approximately 1 to 2 teaspoons should do. After beans have become tender, salt to taste and cook until done to your taste. Serves 8.

STEWED SQUASH AU VIN

3 to 4 pounds fresh, young,
   tender squash
1 green hot pepper or 1½ teaspoon
   Louisiana Hot Sauce
3 large onions
2 or 3 cups sauterne wine

½ cup olive oil
¼ pound salt pork shoulder,
   lean
2 small cloves garlic
Salt
Water, if needed

Peel and cut up squash. Chop onions, not too fine. Dice or press garlic. Cube salt meat in ½ inch squares. Pour olive oil in large iron or heavy aluminum pot. Then put in salt meat and cook until soft, not brown. Place squash, onions, cut up pepper and garlic in pot. Pour wine over squash and salt to taste. Bring to a hard boil and then lower fire and cook slowly until squash has lost its green taste and meat is tender. Takes approximately 1 to 1½ hours. Serves 6 to 8.

If you don' like mustard greens, prepared in this way, you better call you' doctor quick an' fast, 'cause you is sick.

Mos' bes' thing you can do is save that wondermous juice from this, put it in a cup, an' sneak back in the kitchen when no one is watchin' an' drink that you'self!

This juice is call' pot likker an' you' guests gonna wonder how come you come out of that kitchen lickin' you' chops all the time.

Now that the Sout' done rising again, you can get field or Crowder peas in mos' any grocery store in the U. S. an' A.

But when you fixin' these, be sure an don' salt them until they is done. Saltin' them befo' they done make them tough as ol' mule hide.

MUSTARD GREENS AU VIN

4 bunches fresh mustard greens
2 to 3 cups sauterne wine
Olive oil

Salt
Fresh green hot pepper or
Louisiana Hot Sauce

Clean greens well by washing three times. Cover bottom of pot (preferably an iron pot) with about ⅛ inch of olive oil. Place greens in pot and pour wine over them. Put one whole pod of green hot pepper or one teaspoon of Louisiana Hot Sauce (cayenne) in pot. Salt to taste. Cook until greens are tender and seasoning has permeated them. If any additional liquid is needed, add water.

This recipe may also be used for fresh spinach or turnip greens. Serves eight.

Don' forgot to drink the pot likker!

FIELD OR CROWDER PEAS

2 or 3 pounds fresh peas
Olive oil
¼ pound lean salt or pickled
   pork
3 cups sauterne wine

1 large onion
1 small clove garlic
Fresh green hot pepper or 1
   teaspoon Louisiana Hot Sauce
Salt

Shell and wash peas and place in colander to drain. Cover bottom of pot with olive oil. Cube salt meat and fry in olive oil for about 5 minutes. Add peas, then wine. Dice onion and garlic and put into the pot. Add pepper or hot sauce. Add water if any liquid is needed. Cook until peas are tender and done. Salt to taste after peas have become tender.

VARIATIONS: This recipe can be used for fresh butter or lima beans. Frozen beans or peas may be used. Jus' don' shell an' wash 'em. Serves 8.

No doubt you notice that this Irish potato recipe don' say how many it serve. Well, the reason that is is because you should ought to try this before you serve it to company.

Chances is you gonna want to double the recipe when you see how good this is, I garontee.

Company drop' in one us one Sunday an', natcherly, we got to cook for them something.

This here casserole was what come out of the kitchen, after I got through foolin' aroun' out there awhile.

It turn' out so good, now it's a favorite at our house. In fac', it so good I believe you can t'row in you' ol' rubber boot an' not hurt it none, too.

IRISH POTATOES AU GRATIN AU VIN

6 or 8 large potatoes
Olive oil
6 or 8 large onions
1 cup sauterne wine

Red ground cayenne pepper
Salt
3 cups grated American and
    Parmesan or Romano cheese

Cover bottom of casserole with olive oil and rub sides with it. Place in casserole a layer of sliced potatoes, then a layer of sliced onions, and a layer of cheese. Use at least two different types of cheese mixed together. Sprinkle each layer with salt and red pepper to taste. Repeat until casserole is full. Pour wine over the whole mess and bake in oven at about 375 degrees.

CAULIFLOWER OR BROCCOLI AU GRATIN

The above recipe may be used, substituting cauliflower or broccoli for potatoes.

ASPARAGUS WITH SHRIMP CASSEROLE

2 tablespoons olive oil
1 can green asparagus
1½ cups American cheese, grated
½ cup Romano cheese, grated
2 cups boiled peeled shrimp
2 eggs

1 cup sauterne wine
2 teaspoons Worcestershire
1 teaspoon Louisiana Hot Sauce
1½ teaspoon salt
1 can cream of mushroom soup
¾ cup bread crumbs

Put olive oil in bottom of casserole and spread asparagus over it. Then put a layer of American and Romano cheese, topped by a layer of shrimp, topped by another layer of cheese. Continue this process of alternating layers of shrimp and cheese until casserole is ¾ full with a cheese layer on top.

In a bowl, beat the two eggs, gradually adding as you beat, 1 cup of wine. Continue to beat until the mixture smells like eggnog. Add Worcestershire, Hot Sauce and salt and pour over ingredients in casserole. Then pour a can of cream of mushroom soup over the casserole and top with bread crumbs. Bake in hot oven at 350 degrees for one hour. Serves 6.

Here's where you' nose come in handy. When you mixes that wine wit' them egg, you gonna know it's right when the mixture done smell jus' like eggnog at Chris'mus time. But don' drink it, no, you! Put it in the recipe, jus' like I tol' you.

BAKED MACARONI & CHEESE AU VIN

2 12 ounce packages Macaroni
6 eggs
2½ cups grated American
   cheese, per layer
½ cup Romano cheese
2½ cups sauterne wine
1½ teaspoon salt

Strip with Swiss cheese
1½ tablespoon Worcestershire
   sauce
1½ teaspoon green Louisiana
   Hot Sauce (Red, if green not
   available)
Olive oil

Cook Macaroni, drain in colander, wash with cold water.

Grease casserole with olive oil, including sides and bottom.

This casserole is made in layers.

Start with macaroni, add cheeses, and another layer of macaroni, another topping with cheese until casserole is full.

Beat eggs, add wine to beaten eggs, add Worcestershire to this mixture, add green Louisiana hot sauce and salt. Pour this over layered-casserole and add water, if necessary, to barely cover.

Place in oven pre-heated to 350 degrees.

Bake until top layer of cheese is golden brown.

Serves 8.

If any of this is left over - and that ain't likely - chill, cut like fudge and serve as hors d'oeuvres the next day or so.

"Smell them aromas, you! But don' reach out for that yet, or you gonna draw back a stump."

BREADS

HUSH PUPPIES

1 cup corn meal
½ cup flour
1 teaspoon baking powder
1 teaspoon salt

½ teaspoon soda
1 egg, beaten
1 medium onion (chopped fine)
¾ to 1 cup milk or buttermilk

Combine all dry ingredients. Add egg, milk and onions. Mix well. Drop in deep hot fat by spoonsful and brown on all sides.

"Johnny Guitreau, he don' smoke some at all. 'Course, he eat about a dozen of them stogies ever' day, but that don' count none."

HOME-MADE ROLLS A LA ROSINA

3 packages dry yeast
½ cup lukewarm water
   (must not be hot)
1½ cups warm milk (not hot)

4 tablespoons cooking oil
1 tablespoon salt
2 tablespoons sugar
5 or 6 cups of all-purpose flour

Dissolve yeast in water, add milk, oil, salt, sugar. Stir until sugar and salt dissolve.

Put flour into medium size mixing bowl, pour liquid contents into flour and stir until dough becomes rather stiff. Knead by hand until dough is stiff.

Put dough in greased bowl, grease top of dough, set in warm place and let rise until at least double in size (about 45 minutes).

Flour your board, remove dough from bowl to board and knead down.

Pinch off small pieces of dough. Shape into rolls and put on greased cookie sheet, grease top of each roll lightly. Set in warm place and let rise for approximately 35 minutes.

Pre-heat oven to 475 degrees. Place pans on oven rack and bake until golden brown (about 15 minutes).

This recipe will make about 40 lady finger rolls.

HOT WATER CORN BREAD

1 cup corn meal
½ cup flour

1 teaspoon salt
Boiling water

Blend dry ingredients—Add boiling water to make a very stiff batter—By using a spoon make small pones and drop in deep hot grease and brown on all sides.

One of the mos' bes' things about this barbecue sauce is the onions in it.
An' you say to me, "How I gonna know when a onion is done?
An' I gonna told you real quick, "When it don' taste like a raw onion, tha's when!"
In other words, a onion is done when it is sof' and tender, not crunchy.

SAUCES AND GRAVIES

COOKED BARBECUE SAUCE

4 tablespoons olive oil
2 medium onions
2 cloves garlic
½ cup parsley
1 small cayenne pepper, pickled
   or fresh (If not available, ½ -
   ¾ teaspoon Louisiana Hot Sauce)

1 cup sauterne wine
1 tablespoon lemon juice
2 tablespoons Lea & Perrins
1½ teaspoon salt
1 small can tomato sauce
1 teaspoon liquid smoke

Heat olive oil in large sauce pan. Put onions, garlic, parsley, hot pepper in blender. If you don't have a blender, chop real fine. Blend, with just enough water to make it blend. Pour into sauce pan and cook over low flame for about 30 minutes. Add wine, lemon juice, Lea & Perrins, salt, liquid smoke and tomato sauce.

Simmer this entire mixture until onions are done, about an hour, maybe a few minutes more. Cover while simmering. If needed, add water.

"Only eight an' a half pound of them crab? Hell, me, I could eat all that many by mahself, I garontee!"

BARBECUE SAUCE WITH ADDED COMMERCIAL BARBECUE SAUCE

2 teaspoons Louisiana Hot Sauce
4 tablespoons olive oil
4 cups chopped onions (dry onions)
½ cup parsley
1 cup sauterne wine

2 teaspoons Lea & Perrins
2 cloves garlic
1 tablespoon lemon juice
1 cup water
1 teaspoon Liquid Smoke
1 quart commercial barbecue sauce

Follow cooking directions of Barbecue Sauce on Page 85. Add 1 quart of commercial barbecue sauce after this mixture has been cooked for 30 minutes. Simmer for one hour.

SAW MILL GRAVY

This can be made from grease where chicken, rabbit or round steak has been fried. Pour off all but 1 cup of the grease, leaving crumbs. Add flour enough to take up all grease and brown to deep brown. Add milk to make thin gravy, stirring constantly. Salt and pepper to taste. Cook until thickened and serve over bread, cornbread or rice. More milk can be added if it thickens too much.

"You can still get you'self into a big argue in Louisiana about ol' Huey Long. But one thing for sure: Huey wasn' no little man."

DESSERTS

You boun' to notice right off that they ain' no desserts in this cook book, and for ver' good reasons, I garontee!

In the firstes' place, me, I don' like desserts very much at all.

In the secondes' place, me, I sure don' need no desserts, or I'm gonna be big as a house sometime soon.

But mos'ly, they ain' no desserts in this cook book because you don' got no place some at all to put a dessert, after you eat a real Cajun meal!

You gonna get you' plumb satisfy jus' eatin' what's in this cook book.

Also, anyone what wants a dessert, me, I can tell them that the mos' bes' thing they can eat for dessert is maybe a little sherbet, or a dip of ice cream wit' a tablespoon wine or brandy on top.

So you jus' go ahead an' whomp you up a big Cajun meal and then axe you'self if you still want a dessert. If you do, well, it's you' waistline, none of mine. If you don', well, then me, I agree wit' you, I garontee!

— JUSTIN WILSON

89

"Bon appetit! Au revoir!"

The Justin Wilson #2 Cookbook: Cookin' Cajun
Another treasury of Cajun recipes from the kitchen of renowned humorist and gourmet cook Justin Wilson.

The Justin Wilson Gourmet and Gourmand Cookbook
In this tasty collection, the acclaimed gourmet cook shares recipes that will stimulate the most jaded taste buds. Features many of the recipes from Wilson's former PBS show of the same name.

Justin Wilson's Outdoor Cooking with Inside Help
With the aid of a barbecue grill and a "Cajun microwave," you'll be cooking like a Cajun and impressing friends and family with your skills. Includes fifty color photos. Based on the former cooking show of the same name.

Justin Wilson Looking Back: A Cajun Cookbook
The culinary trendsetter takes a look back at his three decades as a Cajun cook and raconteur to select some of his favorite photos and recipes. A companion to the former PBS series of the same name.

Justin Wilson's Easy Cookin': 150 Rib-Tickling Recipes for Good Eating
Justin Wilson, looking for ways to make his cooking easier, eliminates peeling and chopping by using flavored salts and powders instead of onions, celery, and garlic.

··

_____ **The Justin Wilson Cookbook** $9.95 comb
_____ **The Justin Wilson #2 Cookbook: Cookin' Cajun** $9.95 comb
_____ **The Justin Wilson Gourmet and Gourmand Cookbook** $22.00
_____ **Justin Wilson's Outdoor Cooking with Inside Help** $22.00
_____ **Justin Wilson Looking Back: A Cajun Cookbook** $25.00
_____ **Justin Wilson's Easy Cookin': 150 Rib-Tickling Recipes for Good Eating**
          $25.00
_____ **Justin Wilson's Cajun Fables** $16.99, audio CD $15.95
_____ **Justin Wilson's Cajun Humor** $11.95 pb
_____ **More Cajun Humor** $11.95 pb

_____ **Subtotal**
_____ **Postage and handling**
_____ **Sales tax**
_____ **Total enclosed**

Appropriate tax must be included by Louisiana residents. Add $3.95 for 4th-class postage and handling or $7.85 for UPS Ground shipment plus $.75 for each additional copy ordered. Remittance must accompany order.

Name _____

Street _____

City _____ State _____ Zip _____

Pelican Publishing Company, 1000 Burmaster Street, Gretna, Louisiana 70053
··